SUCCESS STORIES
LIBRARY

Burn brightly
without
Burning out

BALANCING YOUR CAREER WITH THE REST OF YOUR LIFE

By Dick Biggs

The unbalanced lifestyle is concerned primarily with *thinking* about, then *doing* whatever is necessary to achieve possessions, power, pleasure and popularity.

The balanced lifestyle, on the other hand, is centered on *being* of sound character and worthwhile purpose, and *having* special joys far greater than possessions, power, pleasure and popularity.

To balance your career with the rest of your life, you must answer life's four greatest questions:

Who am I and why am I here?

Where am I going?

How will I get there?

When I get there, what will I have?

GRAPHICS BY BALANCE DESIGN

Managing Time

Before you manage time, you should manage your dominant interests. These are the major areas of your life where you spend time. Call it personal management, which is what generates your lifestyle focus.

Your dominant interests will vary, so create a unique chart to clarify your lifestyle focus. The ideal number of dominant interests is between 3-7. With less than three, you'll probably be out of balance. With more than seven, you're likely to be stressed out, even burned out.

Don't worry if a particular day is out of balance due to a heavy work load or a family emergency. Strive for weekly, monthly, quarterly or even yearly balance. If you haven't spent time in each area by the end of a year, then reassess your dominant interests or strive for better time management.

Dominant Interests

God, Others, and Personal are subdivided as follows:

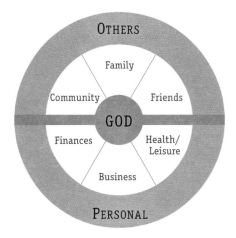

Of course, there is no such thing as perfect balance. There will be days when balance means working longer hours — when balance means spending time with family and friends — when balance means exercising or relaxing — when balance means doing a community project — when balance means handling finances — or when balance means growing spiritually.

Enjoy a better balance between work and the rest of your life by monitoring your number of dominant interests and the amount of activity within each one.

Mission vs.

A mission is "a body of persons sent to perform a service or carry on an activity." Most missions are team efforts and are over once a certain activity is performed i.e., a space mission, military mission, diplomatic mission.

A purpose is a personal, long-term affirmation of what you want "to be." It offers lifetime direction. Use this 10-point model to craft your written purpose statement in as few words as possible:

1. Find a guiding principle as your anchor. (A line from a poem or song, an inspirational quote, a Scripture verse or anything else that sets the tone for your statement.)

2. Make a list of your dominant interests.

3. List the qualities you admire in your role models and mentors.

Purpose

4. State YOUR strongest character qualities.

5. Jot down some key phrases. (Samples: making a difference, leaving a lasting legacy, living with passion, daring to dream, choosing wisely.)

6. Do an outline. (Integrate steps 2-5.)

7. Prepare a rough draft.

8. Edit, rewrite and polish.

9. Share it with a relative or close friend for feedback. (Incorporate any suggestions.)

10. Put the finished document in prominent places.

Image vs.

Image is how others see you and may not be the real you. Integrity is being true to yourself.

To be truthful with others, you must be true to yourself.

Years ago I was conducting a seminar on business ethics in Dallas. A young man flew in from a small town in Arkansas to attend this session.

He'd just been promoted from salesman to sales manager. He sat on the front row, took copious notes, asked questions and couldn't say enough about the importance of ethics in business.

When it was time to catch a cab to the airport, this man asked if we could share a ride and talk more about the day's topic. I agreed. He talked incessantly about the value of my seminar until we arrived at his terminal.

The fare was $40. We each paid $20, but the young sales manager asked the cab driver for a $40 receipt. Pocketing the inflated receipt, he winked and boasted, "I learned that trick from my general manager!"

Integrity

• What other "tricks" had his general manager taught him?

• Would he be teaching these "tricks" to his new sales people?

• Had he heard anything I'd said?

Prior to that revealing moment, my image of this young man was one of integrity. I felt like I'd had a positive impact on him. However, my image changed dramatically when he failed to be true to himself.

The word inteGRITy also includes another word:

Grit — "a firmness of mind, unyielding courage" that leads to...

Respect — "a high or special regard" by others that fosters...

Influence — "which produces an effect without force" based on...

Truth or — "that which agrees with final reality."

Role Modeling vs.

Role models are people you respect for setting worthy examples. Mentors are people who've taken role modeling to the next level by teaching you the details of who they are, how they think, what they've done and why they have something worth pursuing.

In short, master mentors are teachers of life experiences and have these four characteristics:

1. PURSUE WHAT IS TRUE. Who better to help you discover life's timeless truths than mentors who've already struggled with these issues? Mentoring provides a way to shorten your learning curve and accelerate growth through seasoned guides on the job, in the community and within your family.

Mentoring

2. TURN CREEDS INTO DEEDS. Since it's more difficult to model exemplary behavior than recite beliefs, a mentor shows the way and helps you deal more effectively with the struggle "to walk your talk."

3. USE CONGRUENCE TO INFLUENCE. Without congruency between creeds and deeds, there is hypocrisy and no credibility. Mentors can be most influential by providing consistency between words and ways.

4. COLLECTS A DEEP RESPECT. Mentors earn respect through a lifetime of "practicing what they preach." Dr. Michael Guido says that if you remove the "p" from preach, you have reach. If you delete the "r" from reach, you have each. Mentors reach each protege through teaching at a personal level that fosters admiration and emulation.

In the early school years, the focus is on awareness and accumulation of general information to provide an educational foundation and exposure to a variety of career paths. It's the shotgun approach to learning.

Later, the focus shifts to repetition, formation of purpose and application of specialized knowledge because the sheer volume of information makes it impossible to act on every idea. It's the rifle approach to learning.

It's easy to become an education junkie and application flop unless all five steps of knowledge are followed:

1. AWARENESS OF GENERAL INFORMATION. The purpose of awareness is stimulation of thought to alert you to all of life's professional and personal possibilities.

Specialized Knowledge

2. ACCUMULATION OF GENERAL INFORMATION. The purpose of accumulation is to provide a base of learning to serve as your academic foundation.

3. REPETITION OF SPECIALIZED KNOWLEDGE. The purpose of repetition is to gain understanding about a select body of knowledge so you can become an authority in a particular field. The art of mastery is often a gravitation towards a God-given talent.

4. FORMATION OF PURPOSE LINKED TO SPECIALIZED KNOWLEDGE. The bridge between knowledge and action is purpose. Learn all you can about your life's passion (specialized knowledge) to help you discover why you are here (purpose).

5. APPLICATION OF SPECIALIZED KNOWLEDGE. Practice daily what you know and love to do (action) until you become an expert.

Ability vs.

To do your life's work well, you must have ability and skills derived through knowledge and aided by natural aptitude.

Nevertheless, it's your attitude that usually provides the opportunity to use your knowledge, ability and skills in the most enjoyable and meaningful way.

Here are some suggestions for dealing positively with five of life's familiar attitude-busters:

1. PROBLEMS.   Problems are a part of life. Failures complain about their problems and blame everyone else. Successful people become professional problem-solvers and strive to overcome their obstacles by looking for opportunities.

Attitude

2. SELF-PITY.   A self-pitying person asks, "Why me?" and allows a negative attitude to prevail. A self-confident person asks, "How now?" and allows a positive attitude to triumph.

3. WORRY.   Worriers tend to create anxiety about what could happen in the future while endangering their present health through mental distress. Take the attitude that you're too busy acting on today's tasks to worry unnecessarily about tomorrow's troubles.

4. CRITICISM.   Constructive feedback begins with what you did right, proceeds to suggestions for your improvement and ends with a cheerful summary that gives you hope. In seeking feedback, look for people with a caring attitude and ignore critics who offer cruel condemnation.

5. FEAR OF FAILURE.   Your attitude can determine the fine line between success and failure. Did you know that most achievers fail their way to success? Instead of fearing failure, let the power of your attitude keep you focused on success.

Facts vs.

There is no practical value in facts unless you can focus on the wise use of a body of knowledge. Focus, the ability to concentrate on the application of knowledge, comes from doing four things well:

1. Define your purpose.

2. Determine your dominant interests.

3. Develop your goals.

4. Decide on your priorities.

Focus

The Master Plan Funnel Concept™ is a tool for minimizing procrastination and maximizing performance in all areas of living:

Master Plan Funnel Concept™

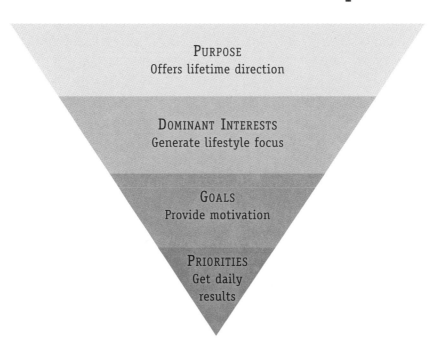

PURPOSE
Offers lifetime direction

DOMINANT INTERESTS
Generate lifestyle focus

GOALS
Provide motivation

PRIORITIES
Get daily
results

When priorities get done daily, goals are eventually realized. When goals are achieved in all of your dominant interests, there is balance. And when there is balance, you're more likely to fulfill your purpose and lead a more meaningful life.

Vision · vs.

A vision ("I have a dream") conveys the big picture of your life, not the details. It's a general, idealistic view of where you'd like to go. Goals are specific, realistic lists of what you intend "to do" on your life's journey.

Goals provide short-term and long-term motivation. Short-term goals can be daily, weekly, monthly, quarterly or annually; long-term goals are beyond a year. Don't concentrate on business goals only. Be balanced and set goals within each of your dominant interests.

Try this "7Rs" goal-setting system:

1. RESPECTABLE. If your goals aren't aligned with the high standards of your purpose statement, why pursue them?

Goals

2. REALISTIC.   Don't set yourself up to fail by creating a large, unrealistic wish list. Succeed by setting fewer, realistic goals as you gain confidence to pursue loftier ambitions.

3. RECORD.   Written goals provide a better system of accountability.

4. REDUCE TO THE SPECIFIC.   The difference between a dream and a goal is a deadline and sense of urgency.

5. REFLECT OFTEN.   Subconsciously, you either see yourself succeeding or failing. Which will it be? Use visualization as a positive reinforcer.

6. RELENTLESSLY PURSUE.   Nothing happens without effort, so go for your goals with gusto.

7. RESPONSIBILITY.   Unforeseeable hardships can ambush your boldest plans. Deal with unexpected challenges such as the death of loved ones, health problems or financial hardships, then resume the quest of your goals or reassess what you want out of life.

Plans vs.

A plan "always implies mental formulation." It's passive.
A priority is "something meriting attention before competing
alternatives." It's active.

Prioritization, the ranking of your
goals in the order of importance, is the
catalyst that sparks daily results.

That's why priorities form the tip of the Master Plan Funnel
Concept. This filtering system allows you to act daily on the most
important things in your career and personal life.

Check off priorities as you achieve them. At night, transfer any
remaining priorities and add new ones to the next day of your calendar. Chip away until a priority is completed, or decide that it's
no longer important and delete it.

Priorities

Use this "5Ds" system for prioritizing your goals:

1. DETERMINE THE IMPORTANCE. Make sure it's really a priority or you can be busy and unproductive.

2. DEADLINE IT. Just like goal-setting, you need a time line to create a sense of urgency.

3. DECIDE ON A PLAN OF IMPLEMENTATION. Don't spend so much time on an action plan that you catch the disease of "paralysis from analysis."

4. DELEGATE IF POSSIBLE. When feasible, assign others with different skills to do what you don't do well.

5. DO IT! Dreaming, learning, planning and talking isn't enough. Eventually, action must be taken if success is to be realized.

Motivation vs.

Motivation is "some inner drive, impulse or intention that causes a person to do something or act in a certain way." Inspiration is "any stimulus to creative thought."

In short, inspiration is about thinking and motivation is about doing.

An inspirer is simply the catalyst or "agent that provokes or speeds significant behavioral change or action." It's up to you to turn inspiration into motivation.

To gain a greater quantity of self-motivation, surround yourself with the greatest quality of inspirers. Here are four ways to increase your inspiration and, in turn, your self-motivation:

Inspiration

1. READ FROM A GOOD BOOK AT LEAST 15-30 MINUTES EACH DAY.

If you're too busy to read for this minimal time each day, could you be too busy?

2. LISTEN TO EDUCATIONAL, UPBEAT AUDIO TAPES EACH WEEK.

This popular form of learning enables you to listen to an interesting message while driving, flying or exercising. The subconscious mind becomes an awesome motivating force as you hear these messages repeatedly.

3. ATTEND AT LEAST ONE WORTHWHILE SEMINAR EACH QUARTER.

One of the most powerful learning tools is a live presentation given by a polished, proficient seminar leader. Look for one or two ideas you can use immediately.

4. DEVELOP A MASTERMIND GROUP THAT MEETS AT LEAST SEMI-ANNUALLY.

This is a relationship comprised of perhaps four to eight positive people willing to offer support, share ideas and provide feedback within a group of your peers at work or elsewhere.

Procrastination vs.

Perhaps the greatest gap in life is the one between knowing and doing. It's the procrastination gap.

Procrastination is the subtle art of sabotaging your potential. The procrastinator spends a lifetime in the twilight zone between thinking and doing. The result is over-analyzing and underachieving.

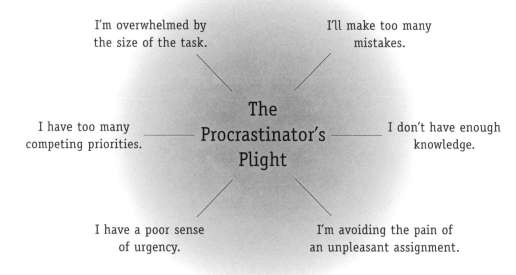

I'm overwhelmed by the size of the task.

I'll make too many mistakes.

I have too many competing priorities.

The Procrastinator's Plight

I don't have enough knowledge.

I have a poor sense of urgency.

I'm avoiding the pain of an unpleasant assignment.

Decisiveness

Be a peak performer on the job and in your life with the help of this five-point model for greater decisiveness:

1. Give careful consideration to all the facts and options. Seek out the advice of experienced people.

2. Pay attention to your heart, intuition and gut feeling. If something makes sense but doesn't feel right, beware.

3. Once you make a decision, don't second-guess yourself. You make too many important decisions in life to waste valuable time lamenting past choices.

4. Act with the knowledge that you'll probably make more good choices than bad ones in a lifetime. Celebrate your good decisions; learn from your mistakes.

5. Anticipate success, but don't be afraid to fail. Ask: What will happen if I don't act? What are the possibilities if I do act? And if for some reason I don't succeed, what's the worst thing that could happen and can I deal with the consequences?

Burn Out vs.

The challenge is to be balanced enough to burn brightly without burning out.

Burn out is the extinguishing of your spiritual, mental, physical or emotional enthusiasm. Within these four areas, burn out often occurs because:

1. A single dominant interest becomes your life — the zealot, workaholic, exercise fanatic, dominating parent, etc.

2. You commit to so many dominant interests that your circuits become overloaded.

Enthusiasm is derived from the Greek word enthouslasmos, which means "to be filled with spirit."

You can't do your best if you don't feel your best. That's why good health is so critical to your peak performance.

Enthusiasm

These *Eight Elite Enhancers Of Longer Life* can help you lessen the risks of burnout and optimize your enthusiasm:

1. Get the proper amount of sleep and relaxation.

2. Have regular, complete preventive medical and dental exams. (A medical exam should include stress and cancer-screening tests.)

3. Eat a balanced, sensible diet and maintain the proper weight.

4. Exercise aerobically, reasonably and consistently.

5. Avoid all tobacco products.

6. Avoid drugs and use alcohol in moderation, if at all.

7. Use home smoke detectors and wear vehicle seat belts.

8. Laugh often, particularly at yourself.

Hard Work vs.

You must develop a core of good habits in order for smart work to precede hard work.

Hard work, a necessity for success, is of no value when directed towards the wrong activity. It's a matter of understanding the difference between activity (being busy) and achievement (being productive).

For example, a smart carpenter measures twice before cutting once. Discipline, the ability to change bad habits into good habits, is what ensures that hard work is directed towards worthwhile achievement.

Albert E. N. Gray, a Prudential Insurance Company executive, was a man who understood the value of discipline in forming good habits. In 1940, he delivered *The Common Denominator Of Success** speech to the Million Dollar Round Table agents attending their convention in Philadelphia.

Good Habits

According to Mr. Gray, "...the secret of success of every person who has ever been successful lies in the fact that they formed the habit of doing things that failures don't like to do." He claimed there's no difference between what failures don't like to do and what successful people don't like to do. The difference? Successful people discipline themselves to do what they don't like to do to get what they really want out of their career and life.

For instance, if you don't form the conscious good habit of setting your alarm clock before going to bed, the unconscious bad habit is that you could oversleep and miss an important business appointment. As Mr. Gray states: "Every single qualification for success is acquired through habit. People form habits and habits form futures."

* If you'd like to have a copy of this remarkable speech, contact the National Association of Life Underwriters at 1922 F Street NW, Washington, DC 20006, 202-331-6086.

Time Strategies

Time strategies deal with the areas where you spend your life and was addressed as managing dominant interests or personal management. Like any strategy, it's a broader plan for how your life will unfold.

Time tactics deal with how you divide each day among your dominant interests. Call it time management. Like any tactic, it provides a more specific method for carrying out a strategy.

How are you spending each day? Are you organized in such a way to maximize this remarkable resource called time? You have 24 hours in each day just like everyone else. Decide which dominant interests will get your attention, then create a time slot on your calendar for every prioritized goal meriting your attention.

vs. Time Tactics

Here are "Ten Terrific Time-Saving Tactics" to help you get more out of each day professionally and personally:

1. Be more focused by using the Master Plan Funnel Concept.

2. Observe the Eight Elite Enhancers of Longer Life.

3. Minimize procrastination by being more decisive.

4. Beware of perfectionism (never finishing).

5. Learn to say NO without feeling guilty.

6. Believe that it's easier to be organized than disorganized.

7. Eliminate costly time-wasters such as needless meetings, excessive interruptions, unnecessary paperwork, etc.

8. Use professional advisors and technology.

9. Make promptness a good habit.

10. Become an exceptional listener.

Desisting vs.

A cease and desist demand is "an order from an administrative agency to refrain from a method of competition or a labor practice found by the agency to be unfair."

Have you ever experienced something that seemed unfair and wanted to quit? Do you know people who are merely existing due to a "cease and desist" mentality?

Generally, if something is worth pursuing in life, the journey will be difficult. That's why you should never underestimate the power of persistence.

One of the best teachers of persistence is your life's critical turning points. Expect to experience 3-9 turning points or "significant changes" in your life. These transitions can be happy experiences like college graduation, work promotions, marriage, children and the start of a business; or unhappy times such as job losses, divorce, financial setbacks, health problems and the death of loved ones.

Persisting

Turning points can provide perspective, which is the ability to view major changes within the larger framework of your lifetime and let the healing power of time prevail. By learning from your turning points, you can grow at a deeper level within your career and life. And isn't persistence all about time and growth?

In the following exercise, list the years of your turning points, what the significant changes were and, if enough time has elapsed, what the long-term impact has been:

YEAR	TURNING POINT	IMPACT
1		
2		
3		
4		
5		
6		
7		
8		
9		

Mastered by Change vs.

Doing your best often means changing. You'll find four unique perspectives on the challenge of change in the following poem:

Will I Master Change Or
Will Change Master Me?

By Dick Biggs

Life's turning points are as sure as the tide
Just a matter of when, so why not decide?
To embrace these transitions as ways to grow
'Tis folly to ignore what you already know.

Make a vow to adapt to the crises of life
There's no reason to suffer more stress and strife.
Quite often change becomes a blessing in time
While making you wiser in pursuit of your prime.

No change is impossible, no one is exempt
You can step out in faith or shrug with contempt.
Life comes in cycles, no two are the same
To claim nothing's new is a naive game.

Mastering Change

Some change is impractical, some things must endure
You need worthwhile values, so profound and pure.
Plus a noble purpose to guide you each day
And give life meaning as you forge your way.

But most things do change, it's a natural law
You can believe this truth or stand there in awe.
It may be uncomfortable, it may cause pain
Won't a regretful heart be a greater strain?

With every change, there's an outcome to bear
So accept the challenge, for life's seldom fair.
Be willing to risk and you're bound to find
More courage and strength from a positive mind.

Be bold, be daring, be receptive to change
For most things are better when you rearrange.
Get out of the rut, seek a new vitality
Move beyond the old to a fresh reality.

Ah, life has turning points, they won't disappear
Rise up to greet them and conquer your fear.
The choice is simple, it's as clear as can be
Will I master change or will change master me?

Stress vs.

Between boring and burn out is a balance based on managing stress by making time for serenity.

Prevention magazine, in an article entitled "Yearning To Be Stress-Free...What Aggravates Americans Most?," conducted a national survey and revealed its Top Ten Stressors:

1. Personal finances
2. Career
3. Too many responsibilities
4. Marriage
5. Health
6. Children
7. Loneliness
8. Sex
9. Relatives
10. Neighbors

Serenity

Frankly, a stress-free life would be boring. Of course, a stressed out life can lead to burn out and worse. Try these suggested stress-relievers to gain more tranquility away from the office:

SPIRITUAL   Depending upon your world view, this can include prayer, meditation, Bible study and active participation at your place of worship; or it might be a walk in nature or a community project.

MENTAL   Whether it's reading, listening to tapes, working cross-word puzzles, writing, playing games or whatever, make time to stimulate your mind apart from work and the daily grind.

PHYSICAL   This might be aerobic exercise like walking, running, hiking, biking or swimming; a team sport like volleyball or basket-ball; or working in the yard or garden.

EMOTIONAL   Options include weekend getaways and vacations; retreats; family reunions; eating out regularly with a group of friends; or having relatives over for dinner to celebrate special occasions.

Urgent vs.

Do you struggle with what you need to do now (urgent) and what you want to do over a lifetime (important)? If so, welcome to the modern world of trying to balance the work you do with the life you lead.

The following exercise may help you appreciate any imbalance you may be experiencing between the urgent and important matters of your life. In the left column, write down all of your urgencies from the past week. In the right column, list what's important during your lifetime:

URGENT (NOW)	IMPORTANT (LIFETIME)

Important

In a typical week, it would be difficult for most of us to write the urgencies of a single day in the small space on the left. However, when I thought about the important matters of a lifetime, my purpose statement came to mind and would almost fit on the right side.

1   I will strive to maintain integrity in all facets of daily living.

2   I will strive to have a positive impact upon the people whose lives I touch; and to set a worthy example to all as a principle-centered role model and mentor.

3   I will strive to honor God in all that I think, say and do. (Purpose statement anchor: Micah 6:8)

Don't let the urgent matters of work sap your energy for the few important matters of a lifetime.

Develop a keen sense of urgency to free up more time to plan and act on the important matters that shape the rest of your life.

Professional Success vs.

Typically, professional success is measured externally by tangible possessions. Personal happiness is measured internally by intangibles such as being true to yourself, touching the lives of others and developing spiritually.

While professional success is a part of your personal happiness, no amount of career achievement can atone for failure in your personal life.

While happiness has been defined in many ways, it can be a lot more difficult to discover. To find more joy in life, consider the "6Fs" and "2Hs" of true happiness:

Personal Happiness

FAITH "To have faith is to be sure of the things we hope for, to be certain of the things we cannot see." HEBREWS 11:1

FREEDOM "Freedom without limits brings chaos." DONALD E. WILDMAN

FAMILY "When families fail, society fails." DAN QUAYLE

FRIENDS "One friend in a life is much, two are many, three are hardly possible." HENRY BROOKS ADAMS

FRATERNALISM "The unselfish love and concern for the welfare of others." WEBSTER'S DICTIONARY

FORGIVENESS "Only the brave know how to forgive...a coward never forgave; it is not in his or her nature." LAURENCE STERNE

HEALTH "The first wealth is health." RALPH WALDO EMERSON

HOPE "There is no medicine like hope, no incentives so great, and no tonics so powerful as the expectation of something better tomorrow." ORISON SWETT MARDEN

Making Money vs.

Making money IS important, but your legacy is even more significant. No matter how much money you earn in a lifetime, these assets become the property of others at your death. However, your legacy will always be yours and the major question is:

Are you making a positive difference with your life?

My parents, Daniel and Thelma Biggs, were Salvation Army officers for 20 years. They didn't make much money, but they made a big difference in the communities where they served. Weirton was one of the towns where my parents left a legacy that really matters.

Captain and Mrs. Biggs served four years in this West Virginia steel town. When they received orders to move to Cumberland, Maryland, it prompted a poignant column by Millie Martin of The Weirton Daily.

In part, she said: "This morning my phone rang off the wall. 'What's this I hear about Captain Biggs leaving?' was the repeated question. Each caller demanded to know why he was being trans-

Making a Difference

ferred and if there was anything that could be done to keep him in Weirton. Once in a while a person moves into a town and, through his noble characteristics, understanding, sympathetic nature, sincere spirit of service and deep interest in his fellow men, enriches the lives of all those with whom he comes in contact. And so it has been with Captain Biggs."

That column was written in 1952, but I didn't learn about it until 40 years later. Carol Johnson, my sister, returned to Weirton to visit some of the people our parents had served. "They were still talking about Captain and Mrs. Biggs," Carol said, "and how much they meant to Weirton."

Joe Powell, a Salvation Army lay leader in this Ohio River community, handed my sister a copy of that newspaper column and introduced her to his son and grandson. Joe had named his son Daniel, who named his son Daniel in honor of our father.

Our parents didn't make a lot of money, but what a tribute to making a difference. They created a legacy in Weirton that's still alive today. What will be your legacy?

SUMMARY

You hold in your hands a small, simple book containing essays, examples and exercises to help you discover a more balanced lifestyle. My wish is that these thoughts will help you balance your career with the rest of your life.

Consider these key points to help you bring your life into balance:

- Monitor your professional life and your personal life and the time you spend on each one of them.
- Anchor your actions with integrity. To be truthful with others, you must be true to yourself.
- Define your priorities. Free up time to plan and act on the important matters of your life.
- Maintain the right attitude. Instead of dwelling on problems and conflicts, let the power of a positive attitude keep you focused on your life's purpose.

- Avoid the plight of procrastination. Be decisive in how you invest your time. Celebrate your good decisions and learn from your mistakes.
- Reflect on the turning points of your life. You will be surprised how much you have grown from past milestones and how powerful these insights can be in planning your future.
- Understand that professional success is a part of your personal happiness, but no amount of career achievement can atone for failure in your personal life.

Your objective should be to gradually improve the balance between your professional success and your personal happiness. The challenge is to identify a healthy balance between work and the rest of your life – to burn brightly without burning out.

 As president of Biggs Optimal Living Dynamics (BOLD!), Dick Biggs works with organizations to boost their bottom lines (sales and profits) and better their top lines (people and productivity.) ☞ His professional development topics include programs on sales, marketing, leadership, writing and speaking skills. His personal growth topics include programs on balanced living, stress management, time management and change. He serves Fortune 500 companies, associations, government agencies and professions such as dentistry, banking, insurance and real estate. ☞ Since 1986, Dick has been a keynote speaker and seminar leader, producing results for clients in 37 States, Canada, England, Germany and Guam. He's also the author of "If Life Is A Balancing Act, Why Am I So Darn Clumsy?"... producer of "How To Balance Your Life," a six-cassette audio album... and editor of "Balanced Living Digest," a quarterly newsletter. ☞ Dick is a member of the National Speakers Association and a past president of the Georgia Speakers Association. He's a former Marine embassy guard in Warsaw and Rome and veteran marathon runner. His early career included stints as a sports writer for The Atlanta Constitution and staff writer for the Associated Press. ☞ Dick is married and lives on the shores of beautiful Lake Lanier just north of Atlanta. He's active in his church as a Sunday school teacher.

To inquire about Dick's services and products, please contact him at:
Biggs Optimal Living Dynamics (BOLD!),
9615 Settlers Lane, Gainesville, GA 30506

PHONE 770-886-3035 FAX 770-886-3017
E-MAIL: biggspeaks@mindspring.com
WEB PAGE: biggspeaks.home.mindspring.com

The cost is low...
but the ideas are priceless!

Each title in the Successories "Power of One" library takes less than 30 minutes to read, but the wisdom it contains will last a lifetime. Take advantage of volume pricing as you share these insights with all the people who impact your career, your business, your life.

Anatomy of A Leader
This collection of insights written by Carl Mays represents a simple thought-provoking body of knowledge that can help everyone develop the qualities of a leader. #713259

Attitude: Your Internal Compass
Denis Waitley and Boyd Matheson give powerful examples of how a slight shift in the way you see the world can yield powerful results in an ever-changing workplace. #713193

Burn Brightly Without Burning Out
This book, by motivational expert Dick Biggs, will boost morale and productivity by helping people balance the work they do with the life they lead. #716016

Companies Don't Succeed...People Do
Successories founder and Chairman, Mac Anderson, outlines "The Art of Recognition" – how to develop employees and a recognition culture within any organization. #716015

Dare to Soar
The spirit of eagles inspired this unique collection of motivational thoughts by noted speaker Byrd Baggett. Any goal can be reached if you "Dare to Soar." #716006

The Employee Connection
Noted employee motivation expert Jim Harris provides dozens of practical methods for leaders to "unleash the power of their people." #716018

Empowerment
Ken Blanchard and Susan Fowler Woodring's valuable insights into empowerment outlines how to achieve "Peak Performance Through Self-Leadership." #716022

Motivating Today's Employees
Recognition expert Bob Nelson offers a great primer on the impact of employee rewards and recognition. #716007

Motivating Yourself
Mac Anderson, Successories founder and Chairman, offers a mix of proven ideas and motivational thoughts to help "Recharge the Human Battery." #716021

Motivation, Lombardi Style
Use the coach's memorable collection of insights about the athletic playing field and the business battlefield to inspire your team. #716013

Pulling Together
Nationally-noted author and speaker, John Murphy, outlines "17 Principles for Effective Teamwork" with a refreshing mix of information and thought-provoking questions. #716019

Quality, Service, Teamwork
Share these "Foundations of Excellence" with your employees! This valuable resource includes over 100 motivational quotes. #716014

Results
Help your sales team turn passion into profit and maximize their relationship power with these proven strategies for changing times. Jeff Blackman's experience and style makes this an entertaining handbook that guarantees results. #716017

Rule #One
Author and customer service expert C. Leslie Charles has compiled dozens of insightful ideas, common sense tips and easy-to-apply rules in this customer service handbook. #716008

Teamwork
Noted consultant Glenn Parker gives managers, team leaders and members a valuable blueprint for successful team building. Put it to work for your team! #716012

Think Change
This intriguing book, by John Murphy, challenges today's employees to change their thinking to keep up with an evolving workplace. "Adapt and Thrive or Fall Behind." #716020